First published 2015 by Retro Inc Books
www.nickmackie.co.uk
Illustrations & Text copyright © 2015 Nick Mackie

ISBN 978-09563290-42

Jeremy Corbyn was born on May 26th, 1949.

Chippenham, England

Some of the press have criticised Jeremy
for being unpatriotic and a possible security threat.

Help Jeremy become more British

ELVIS PRESLEY

If I can dream

Jeremy is a fan of Elvis

BATMAN

Corbyn - The caped crusader

HOBBIES

Jeremy is a keen cyclist.

Help him win the yellow jersey.

BOB DYLAN

The times they are a changin' (possibly)

Jeremy is a fan of Bob Dylan

THE MARX BROTHERS

Groucho, Harpo or Karl ?

JAMES BOND

Dr. No

Not on her Majesty's secret service service

Jeremy is a keen Arsenal supporter.

Help him get onto the team.

Jeremy is a drain-spotter.
He enjoys photographing cast iron street furniture
such as manhole covers and drainage grids.

Help him become a successful operculist.

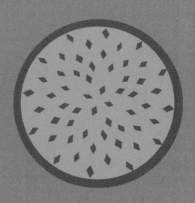

CHARLIE CHAPLIN

The Champion or The Tramp

DR WHO

Help Jeremy become The Doctor

Lion tamer, Unicorn whisperer

SANTA

What will Santa bring you this Christmas?

1: Stick the images onto card

2: Cut out

3: Assemble parts

(Glitter optional)

More info & downloads at:
retroinc.co.uk

Author website:
nickmackie.co.uk

ISBN 978-09563290-42

Printed in Great Britain
by Amazon